K-POP

KOREAN CULTURE NO.2

K-POP: A New Force in Pop Music

Copyright © 2011
by Korean Culture and Information Service

First Published in 2011 by
Korean Culture and Information Service
Ministry of Culture, Sports and Tourism

Phone: 82-2-398-1914~20
Fax: 82-2-398-1882
Website: www.kocis.go.kr

ISBN: 978-89-7375-166-2 04600
ISBN: 978-89-7375-163-1 (set)

Printed in the Republic of Korea

For further information about Korea, please visit:
www.korea.net

K-POP

A New Force in Pop Music

Contents

The K-pop bands, which include (from far left) T-ara, Mblaq and T-Max, gathered on stage for the finale to sing Michael Jackson's Heal The World. ST PHOTOS: SAM CHIN

-pop for a good cause

n groups thrilled
rowd with catchy
s and helped raise
for Mercy Relief

concert

THE WORLD

Singapore Expo

Girl group
Afterschool
(left) showed
off their long
lean legs in
their short
shiny dresses.

stage to deafeni
of pyrotechnics

Clad in sma
members, all sp
ly fast songe
Ye

for seven-memb

ional

r new breed of Korean pop

Photograph: Toshifumi Kitamura/AFP

EVENING STANDARD MONDAY 3 OCTOBER 2011

Trend Spot
weet taches

ready for "Movember"
these limited-edition
late moustaches
ble at Selfridges
99 each

EAT SIX COURSES FOR £19 AT THE ENGLISH LAUNDERETTE'S SIXTIES THEMED DINNER UNTIL OCTOBER 16 ENGLISHLAUNDERETTE.CO.UK

Trends
35

K-POP CRAZY

Mass interest on social networking sites
and a kitsch designer image make
South Korean pop the latest fixation for
London's teens, says **Victoria Stewart**

ly on the
neighbour-
aurants and
stralia.
rote since she
ntry by Korean
From the overly
ng popular Japanese
forming Musumi.
bands look more pro-
"Japanese singers are
next door in the way they
But Korean singers are bet-
more sophisticated."
s, the 28-year-old adds,
idifferent than J-pop groups
Asian identity. "J-pop female
cute, but in a very Japanese
cute)way," she says. "K-pop sing-

ers have a more Asian feel to them. That
appeal to me. And their fans here appreci-
ate that attempts to learn Japanese."
   The linguistic nod makes commercial
sense. Japan is the second biggest music
market in the world after the US, with a
22% global share, according to the International Federation of the Phonographic
Industry. CD sales in South Korea are one
30th of those in Japan.
   K-pop artists have taken localisation
to its natural conclusion: in their native
South Korea, Tobo Shinki are known as
Dong Bang Shin Ki, while the rest of the
world knows them as TVXQ. Girls' Generation perform in Japan as Shojo Jidai, and in
South Korea as Soyuh Nyuh Sni Dae,
Stephen McClure, the Tokyo-based
editor of McClure's Asia Music News,

attributes some of K-pop's p
stylistic differences with its
ticated' J-pop counterpart.
   South Korean manageme
invest considerable time an
loring their acts to the Jap
McClure adds, "The band
incredible effort to learn
game, they do all the
endorsements and app
music shows. They ha
very marketable produ
nese template for idol
   The K-pop wave
land and Malaysia, is
of interest in the U
Europe, if anyone
make it internatio
artist," says McCl

Generation performing in Tokyo this year

Kisetore premium: girl teen
band 2NE1 are part of a wave of
South Korean bands to generate
millions of YouTube hits

he seven "Big Bang
dddb... girl's
ide the PSY, the
s and to betoch
s the 201 release
But pop, as of
South Korean mus

YouTube, thousands of views on a
lonely. And part of course of you
South Korean Pop

YouTuber
Aorean music and is based it's
Additional read

Roo
to
aff

Re

Pop goes the whistle again

K-pop is an industry in South Korea and
and what's more, it's coming to the UAE!

THE TIGER
t stands
FIRM

IV South Korea
Capital: Seoul

All about
SOUTH

Area 96

W

L

PROLOGUE

In October 2009, the Korean girl group 2NE1's album *To Anyone* ranked second after Eminem's *Recovery* on the Top Hip Hop Albums chart on iTunes, the largest online music vendor in the United States.

At a concert hall in Los Angeles, five hundred Girls' Generation fans wearing T-shirts that read "Soshified"—"Soshi" is a shortened form of "Sonyeo Shidae," the Korean name of the girl group—sang the group's song "Gee" while performing a synchronized dance to the music. The YouTube video of the popular Girls' Generation song "Gee" had more than 56 million hits as of October 2011.

In June 2011, young fans came from all over Europe—the UK, Germany, Spain, Italy, Sweden, and elsewhere—to see Korean idol groups including TVXQ!, Super Junior, SHINee, Girls' Generation, and f(x) at Le Zénith de Paris in France, a venue where many famous European pop acts have held concerts.

In Bangkok, Thai youngsters dreaming of becoming "the next Nichkhun" (a member of boy band 2PM) hold singing and dancing competitions to Korean music every weekend.

What do all of these happenings around the world have in common? The answer is "K-Pop."

Girls' Generation, one of the most popular K-Pop girl groups overseas / Source: SM Entertainment

What is K-Pop?

It was in the mid-1990s that Korean pop music first began gaining wider international attention under the name of "the Korean Wave," or "Hallyu" in Korean. The term "K-Pop"—an abbreviation for "Korean pop"—entered wide use overseas during this period, when Korean pop groups such as H.O.T. started to win over the massive Chinese youth audience. As Korean pop singers, with training under major entertainment agencies, went through a process of trial and error, K-Pop continued gaining recognition in

other parts of the world. In the late 2000s, it began spreading beyond the regions of China, Japan, and Southeast Asia and into Europe and the United States. It is increasingly gaining recognition as something more than just a fad—as a phenomenon that has staying power with global audiences.

Defining what K-Pop really is, however, can be somewhat tricky. Is it Korean pop music made by Koreans, or sung and performed by Korean artists? Can it include pop music made and sung by non-Koreans who perform in Korea? The increasing presence of global producers and composers on the K-Pop scene has blurred the criteria somewhat, but if we take into account the fact that K-Pop began receiving serious attention from the global audience in the wake of the overseas success of Korean pop groups, we may define K-Pop here as Korean pop music sung and performed by Korean artists and received positively by international fans.

The K-Pop songs that are most popular with international audiences have several key factors that make them unique and catchy. One of the most common forms of the K-Pop song features a repetitive chorus with a synchronized group dance. Representative examples of this kind of song include "Nobody" by the Wonder Girls, "Gee" by Girls' Generation, "Ring Ding Dong" by SHINee, and "Mister" by KARA. Overseas fans of K-Pop copy the group dances and upload the videos onto YouTube, which promotes the rapid spread of K-Pop music.

On the Global Stage

Korean singer BoA, a major success in Japan
Source: SM Entertainment

The increase in international media coverage of K-Pop has been visible. On June 1, 2002, the French daily *Le Monde* ran a feature story on female Korean singer BoA, who was actively involved in both the Korean and Japanese pop scenes. "With a talent combining a powerful voice, singing, and dancing, BoA became the first singer from the Korean peninsula who pulled off a success in Japan," the article said. Going into detail on how the Korean Wave and K-Pop had hit Southeast Asia, the newspaper said, "BoA's success suggests that the youth of Korea and Japan, who do not possess their predecessors' anger toward each other, will be closer than in the past. She has served as a more effective bridge between the two countries than decades of diplomatic efforts."

The business weekly *Forbes* picked K-Pop as one of the "20 Trends Sweeping The Globe" in 2008. In the article, it said, "Korean pop music has made waves across Asia for years, with homegrown stars selling out shows from Kyoto to Kuala Lumpur."

In its incipient stages, Korean pop music was strongly influenced by Western pop music, diversifying through many stages of copying, translation, and interpretation from the early 20th

Forbes article describing K-Pop as one of the top trends sweeping the globe

British fans holding pictures of Korean artists

century. Those unique creations by experimental and creative Korean artists are now being received by international audiences in the form of K-Pop. That being said, K-Pop's increasing popularity around the world is part of a cultural exchange in the context of human history. As a tool for exchange between East and West, K-Pop belongs not only to Korea but to the world.

This book starts by examining current trends in K-Pop, which swept the Asian market over a short period of time starting in the mid-1990s and is now looking to the world's largest pop market in the United States. Next, it will examine the question of why K-Pop has become popular around the world. The book will explain in detail how appealing cultural content wrapped in the K-Pop package is reaching every corner of the globe, reaching beyond barriers of language and geography through the tools of new media. In the following chapter, the book will cover how K-Pop has been shaped in the context of Korean pop culture history. Although the K-Pop songs currently enjoying popularity overseas are mostly dance numbers by Korean idol groups, Korean pop music hosts a far wider range of genres and an interesting history to boot. In the last chapter, the book will look at the K-Pop artists who have enjoyed the most popularity in recent years.

European fans calling for K-Pop concert in London's Trafalgar Square

Chapter One

K-POP MEETS THE WORLD

A news report, dated June 22, 2011, by the Korean daily *Dong-A Ilbo* featured an interesting graphic. It was a global map of K-Pop popularity, created by analyzing the number of hits on the YouTube channels of the country's three largest entertainment agencies and seeing where the hits came from. With deep colors used to represent where the hits were numerous and pastel colors to show where they were fewer, K-Pop's popularity was presented on a single map of the world.

In the map, the colors were deepest for Korea, Japan, and Southeast Asia, indicating that fans in those regions were clicking most on the YouTube video clips of their favorite K-Pop artists. The next deepest colors were seen in the US, followed by China, Canada, Australia, South America, Europe, Russia, and Africa.

Among the official K-Pop videos streamed on entertainment agency channels, Girls' Generation's video for "Gee" had surpassed 56 million hits as of October 2011. With the exception of a few countries in Africa, people from all over the world had viewed the video on YouTube at least once, the report said.

In an article on June 11, 2011, *Sisa Journal* said that the Korean Wave was riding on the "Digital Silk Road"—a new way of sharing cultural content beyond barriers of race, culture, and region. Now, this globalization of K-Pop has moved from its Internet beginnings onto offline platforms throughout the world.

K-Pop Makes a Splash in Europe

A number of K-Pop concerts have been staged overseas in the past several years, but it was the SMTOWN LIVE WORLD TOUR in PARIS, held at Le Zénith de Paris on June 10 and 11, 2011, that marked a significant turning point in K-Pop's impact on Europe. A single concert had originally been

Fans go wild for Girls' Generation at the SMTOWN LIVE WORLD TOUR in PARIS.

planned for June 10, but the agency SM Entertainment decided in May to add another show on June 11 after hundreds of French K-Pop fans rallied in Paris for an extra concert.

Their demand—in the form of a flash mob and group dance to a K-Pop soundtrack—came after tickets for the June 10 concert, priced from 45 euro ($65) to 200 euro ($280) in a 7,000-seat venue, sold out in just 15 minutes. Numerous media reports noted the significance of the flash mob protests, remarking that Korean idol groups were holding their first concert in Paris at the request of French fans, and the French rallies in front of the Louvre Museum, a symbol of French cultural pride, resulted in an extra K-Pop show.

The idol groups appearing at the concerts included TVXQ!, Super Junior, Girls' Generation, SHINee, and f(x), who later expressed joyful astonishment upon their arrival at Charles de Gaulle Airport when a crowd of some 1,500 fans from France, the UK, Italy, Switzerland, and elsewhere in Europe welcomed them with flowers and banners.

Flash mob requesting a Polish concert by K-Pop artists

The flash mobs in Paris have become a watershed, followed by others planned by fans in other cities and regions of the world, including London, New York, Mexico, and Peru, all of them calling for more K-Pop concerts. On July 10, European fans from various countries gathered in Trafalgar Square in central London and danced to the Korean pop tune "Fire," a hit from the girl group 2NE1.

British fans cheer in front of the Abbey Road Studios in London where Korean boy group SHINee held a special concert for music industry officials and the press.

Holding a banner reading "Bring YG to the UK," the fans delivered unison renditions of "Tonight" by Big Bang, "I Am the Best" by 2NE1, "Digital Bounce" by Se7en, and "High High" by GD & TOP—all in the original Korean—and performed synchronized group dances to the music. Britons passing by asked about the meaning of "YG" and learned that it was the name of the Korean entertainment agency responsible for the idol groups whose performance the UK fans were requesting at the Thames Festival in September.

Yonhap News quoted a 17-year-old British Muslim saying that she had learned about K-Pop through YouTube videos and made friends with Koreans. "I hope the YG singers can come to the UK," she said. "I also hope K-Pop singers can become world superstars."

The increased British interest in K-Pop was apparent in early 2011 when the Korean Cultural Center UK held a "K-Pop Night" event in February. The center had only advertised the event through Facebook, but word of mouth resulted in a turnout of 620 people, some of whom had traveled five to six hours by train to attend the event.

K-Pop's Appeal? Novelty

An interview with Katie Kim

Katie Kim, who emigrated to Great Britain with his family at the age of nine, orchestrated the July 2011 flash mob in Trafalgar Square to call for a K-Pop performance. Kim put up a Facebook message proposing that people hold a flash mob to ask for a UK performance by YG Entertainment acts, which was met with an enthusiastic response from numerous European K-Pop fans.

How popular is K-Pop in the UK?

K-Pop fans are generally aged 14 to 20, so we can't really say K-Pop consumption has reached the "mass" level. But it gets burned into your brain from just one listen, and I think that if there are more opportunities to listen to the music offline, through performances and such, then it will be able to move outside the Internet and go public.

Why does the K-Pop fan base center on the younger generation?

It's the novelty. British music gets old fast because of the similarity, and J-Pop has been losing its scarcity value because it's so easily accessed. But K-Pop is currently something of "mystery." People see the dynamic music and the unfamiliar language of Korean as something fresh. And while there are a lot of bands in the UK, it's hard to find idol groups with strong music, performances, looks, and fashion.

What is behind the popularity of YG's musical acts?

It's because the music is based in hip hop and R&B. We think the music of YG's singers strikes a good balance between Western and Eastern. The music and the videos lose nothing when compared with the UK's.

(Adapted from an interview by Wang Eun-jeong at Yonhap News)

After the concert requests in Paris and London, a company in Moscow asked for a concert of K-Pop artists affiliated with Cube Entertainment. The agency was planning to hold the United Cube Concert in London in November 2011, featuring such artists as 4Minute, BEAST, and G.NA, after an August concert with the same lineup in Japan. Industry officials said a K-Pop concert in Moscow would lead to growing popularity for K-Pop in Eastern Europe.

US Starts to Notice K-Pop

The Wonder Girls was the first K-Pop act to make a meaningful impact on the US pop market, the world's largest. While the group was turning out consecutive hits in Korea with "Tell Me" in 2007 and "Nobody" in 2008, it was simultaneously preparing to make its debut in the US market. In early 2009, the group went on a world tour, visiting Bangkok, Los Angeles, and New York, and its agency later announced that the Wonder Girls would be joining the Jonas Brothers' world tour in 2009.

The Wonder Girls came to the attention of the US as an opening act on the Jonas Brothers' world tour.

The group officially released an English version of "Nobody" in the summer of 2009, just before joining the Jonas Brothers' tour in North America. The song made it onto the Billboard Hot 100 in October 2009, making the group the first Korean artists ever to enter the chart.

Around the same time in October 2009, another powerful K-Pop girl group, 2NE1, was storming

Source: JYP Entertainment

the music chart on iTunes, one of the largest music retailers in the United States. Just behind to the top-ranking album *Recovery* by Eminem, 2NE1's album *To Anyone* stood at No. 2 on the iTunes Hip Hop album chart. The group's success in iTunes album sales was quite formidable, considering that the group had never promoted their album overseas.

More recently, Taeyang, a member of boy band Big Bang, became the first Asian artist to reach No. 3 on the iTunes R&B/Soul chart and No. 1 on the Canadian R&B/Soul chart with his solo album, *Solar International*, in July 2011. This was a significant achievement in that a Korean pop singer had made a notable move in the world's largest R&B music market. His album's initial shipment was 30,000 units, which sold out in a single day.

Taeyang's solo album *Solar International* reached No.3 on the iTunes R&B/Soul chart.

With an increasing number of Korean pop acts gaining popularity among US fans, other people in the country who had not been exposed to Korean culture began recognizing K-Pop as well. To spur American interest in K-Pop and draw more attention to contemporary Korean culture, the Korean Cultural Service New York and the Korean pop culture news site allkpop.com hosted the New York K-Pop Contest on July, 2011, at Central

English-Language K-Pop Websites

When K-Pop idol groups hold concerts overseas, the front seats are almost always reserved first by local fans who sing along with the songs in Korean, even though they rarely speak the language. These fans find all kinds of information about idol groups online, including their concert schedules, events, album releases, online music releases, and fan meetings.

Several websites are available to provide quick and accurate K-Pop information for English speakers. Allkpop.com is one of the largest of these sites. Launched by a second-generation Korean-American in 2007, the site has become a major source for the latest K-Pop news. According to Google data, the site has a registered membership of over 300,000, with as many as 3 million monthly visitors. About 36 percent of the members are Asian, followed by 28 percent Caucasian, 24 percent Hispanic, and 10 percent African-American.

Soompi.com is another popular site offering K-Pop celebrity news and other Korean pop culture updates for English-speaking Internet users. As of January 2011, it was drawing some 1.4 million visitors a day, more than 90 percent of them

Park's Naumburg Bandshell for the second annual "Korea Day." The contest was an opportunity for anyone residing in the US to showcase their skills at singing and/or dancing to their favorite K-Pop songs.

The event was a test bed for seeing whether K-Pop's success in Paris would continue in the United States. A contest was held among a thousand or so young Americans, New Yorkers, Facebook K-Pop fan club members, and tourists, with 15-year-old Madison Gunst emerging as the victor. Gunst, who said she harbors ambitions of becoming the first non-Asian K-pop idol, was awarded one round-trip ticket to Korea to participate in the Korean International K-Pop contest slated for November later that year.

non-Koreans. Headed by CEO Joyce Kim and based in San Francisco, Soompi. com plays like a social hub for fans of Korean pop culture. In an interview with a Korean daily in early 2011, Kim said 99 percent of the content was user-generated.

Kokokoreano.com is centered more on K-Pop celebrity fashion, but it also offers important K-Pop news. While providing details on how top K-Pop stars dress at fashion shows, on the street, or at the airport, the site also uploads the latest music videos and live performances by K-Pop stars.

K-Pop Stars Break Records in Japan

Music Bank at Tokyo Dome was co-hosted by Hyun Woo (Middle) and two members of KARA, Gyu-ri (Left) and Hara (Right)

On July 13, 2011, an army of K-Pop artists performed at Tokyo Dome as part of Korean broadcaster KBS's pop music program *Music Bank*. According to news reports, more than 45,000 fans in Japan gathered at the venue, a landmark for concerts in Japan, to enjoy the K-Pop performances.

A Japanese fan was quoted as saying that she had first watched Korean dramas (miniseries) and listened to Korean music, and that her interest had grown to the point where she was now enjoying Korean food.

While K-Pop has enjoyed fast success around the world, its Japanese success is remarkable in that the pop market there is the world's second largest, after that of the United States. In the late 2000s, K-Pop was taken to the next level in Japan. While solo artist BoA and boy bands like TVXQ!, also known as Dong Bang Shin Ki in Korean, had entered the market by making their debuts from scratch and performing in Japanese in the early and mid-2000s, girl groups like Girls' Generation and KARA gained

(Left) TVXQ! was the first Korean boy band to hit it big in Japan. (Right) Japanese fans hold a banner reading "Tohoshinki," the Japanese name of TVXQ!.

popularity in the later part of the decade by recording Japanese versions of their songs that had originally enjoyed popularity in the Korean market.

Several Korean girl groups have had successful debuts and performed on television entertainment shows in Japan, but Girls' Generation has been especially big in the Japanese pop market. The nine-member girl group saw its first Japanese album *Girls' Generation* sell more than 500,000 units within a month after its release. The album was certified double platinum by the Recording Industry Association of Japan, a first for a Korean female pop group.

The album also ranked first on Japan's Oricon weekly album chart on June 7 after selling 232,000 copies in the first week of June 2011. Oricon said this was the highest-ever sales for a foreign act releasing its debut album in the country. Girls' Generation held its first Japanese arena tour in 2011, traveling to six cities to perform for over 140,000 fans.

Another girl group, KARA, broke a record with its fourth single, "Go Go Summer," selling 114,000 copies within the first week of its release on July 11, 2011. Just three weeks later, their single "Jet Coaster Love" sold 123,000 copies within the first week, giving the girl group consecutive first-week single sales exceeding 100,000 copies. It was the first time in the 44-year history of the Oricon singles chart that a foreign female act had accomplished this.

The members of KARA have appeared frequently on Japanese TV—even starring in their own miniseries, *URAKARA*.

Unlike Girls' Generation, which intentionally limited its appearances on TV, KARA actively appeared on Japanese entertainment programs and game shows. The two groups have contrasting images and characters: Girls' Generation goes for a strong, sexy, professional image, while KARA shows off the members' cute, innocent, and feminine sides. The five members of KARA also starred in the 12-episode Japanese miniseries *URAKARA* in early 2011. The show, a fictionalization of the group's experiences, aired on the major Japanese broadcaster TV Tokyo.

The string of K-Pop successes in the Japanese album market has led the Japanese media describe the phenomenon as a "Korean Invasion," just as the US experienced a "British Invasion" of rock in the 1960s with such acts as the Beatles and the Rolling Stones.

K-Pop Triggers New Hallyu in Southeast Asia

The Korean Wave, or Hallyu, can be divided into two stages chronologically. The first lasted from 1997 to the early 2000s. During this period, the wave was taking shape primarily in China, Taiwan, and Vietnam, with such new Korean miniseries as *What Is Love All About* and K-Pop performed by idol groups like H.O.T. The second stage began in the late 2000s, and K-Pop in Southeast Asia played a leading role in triggering the "Neo-Korean Wave,"or the "new Hallyu," with Korea's pop music serving as the major driving force behind the global audience's craving for Korean culture.

Most Southeast Asian countries have homegrown pop music that accounts for more than 50 percent of the overall market, but a variety of Korean idol groups—both male and female—are seeing their albums and songs shooting up the different album and single charts. Super Junior's

K-Pop Drives Hallyu Craze

According to a June 2011 survey, K-Pop is the key factor in the growing popularity of the Korean Wave overseas, and Asian women in their 10s to 20s make up the majority of overseas Hallyu fans. The Korea Tourism Organization conducted the online Hallyu survey on its website (www.visitkorea.or.kr), with responses from 12,085 non-Korean visitors from 102 countries between May 11 and 31, 2011. The survey asked seven questions on the Korean Wave in seven languages—English, Japanese, traditional and simplified Chinese, German, French, Spanish, and Russian—on the site, through e-mail and on social networking services such as Twitter and Facebook.

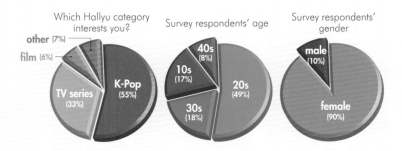

Which Hallyu category interests you?
other (7%)
film (6%)
TV series (33%)
K-Pop (55%)

Survey respondents' age
40s (8%)
10s (17%)
20s (49%)
30s (18%)

Survey respondents' gender
male (10%)
female (90%)

When asked to select the category of Hallyu that interested them, 55 percent of the respondents, or 6,447 people, picked K-Pop. This was followed by TV series with 33 percent, film with 6 percent, and "other" with 7 percent. A breakdown by age showed 49 percent of respondents to be in their 20s, followed by 18 percent in their 30s, 17 percent in their 10s, and 8 percent in their 40s. Some 90 percent of respondents (10,826) were female. Interest in Hallyu celebrities differed among language groups. English speakers favored Super Junior, while French and Spanish users preferred Big Bang. Japanese users in their 40s and 50s showed more interest in TV series than in K-Pop, and Japanese respondents in their 20s and 30s were most interested in K-Pop.

album *Bonamana* held down the top spot on Taiwan's Korean Music Top 100 for 63 consecutive weeks from the first week of June 2010 to the first week of August 2011, breaking the group's own record on the chart, which is displayed on kkbox, Taiwan's largest online music site (http://tw.kkbox.com). This chart supremacy over a year was the longest among any artists in the world appearing on the chart. In 2010, the group's third album, *Sorry Sorry*, topped the same chart for 36 weeks.

Meanwhile, Super Junior-M, a subunit of Super Junior targeting the Chinese music industry with a mix of Korean and ethnically Chinese members, made its 2008 debut in Asian countries including China. Released in Chinese in February 2011, its EP *Taiwanmei* (*Perfection*) was well received by young people, and the group drew more than 6,000 fans to its "2011 *Taiwanmei* Taiwan Fan Party" on June 6, 2011.

Super Junior, a leading group in Southeast Asia's "New Hallyu"

Source: SM Entertainment

The K-Pop craze in Southeast Asia is unique in that it has become common to see K-Pop imitations by local entertainers. As K-Pop provided the driving force for the new Hallyu with its focus on idol groups, Southeast Asian entertainers began to model themselves on the groups' songs and concepts and use similar names. Their existence became widely known to South Koreans with a report on by the KBS program *Entertainment Weekly* on November 6, 2010.

Super Junior-M's EP *Taiwanmei* (*Perfection*)was released in Chinese.

The first act introduced was the Thai female quartet Candy Mafia, who modeled on the K-Pop group 2NE1. This was followed by Ring Ding Dong in Cambodia modeled on SHINee, Idol Girls in China modeled on Girls' Generation, and OK-Bang in China modeled on Big Bang. Some of them even made debuts as official groups, with their perfect imitations of costumes and group dances. "In countries where there is no system to bring together experts from different areas to nurture idol groups, people will see Korean idol groups as a nice and cool trend, something they want to copy," music critic Seong Woo-jin was quoted as saying in the report.

Chapter Two

WHY **K-POP?**

Japanese pop music, also known as "J-pop," was a trend among the youth of Asia in the 1990s, with its commercial peak coming in the late 1990s. Now, however, the attention of the international audience including Asian youth is moving toward K-Pop, which has seen its impact on the planet growing continuously for more than a decade. What makes K-Pop so attractive to worldwide audiences? What are the decisive factors that define K-Pop in its current state, and why is its popularity surging?

The popular weekend program *Monocle* on the 24-hour Bloomberg TV network featured a special report on Korea's music industry and K-Pop on February 20, 2011. The program addressed three aspects of K-Pop's competitiveness. First, it pointed out that K-Pop is a real business with strong export potential. Second, the program said social media played a significant role in K-Pop's success. Third, it noted that K-Pop is not just music but a combination of audio and visual impacts.

Hybrid Entertainment

Because much of K-Pop is centered on music sung and performed by idol groups, K-Pop's international popularity should be analyzed based on these groups' music.

With that in mind, Lee Dong-yeon, a professor at Korea National University of Arts, commented on the transnational musical style of Korean idol pop in his book *Idol: From H.O.T. to Girls' Generation, Cultural Report on Idols*, which was co-authored by various critics and professors. "Although Korean idol pop music borrows the styles of American hip hop and Euro techno," Lee said in the book, "it doesn't copy them wholesale." H.O.T. and Sechs Kies, the two rival idol groups in the 1990s, mixed their sounds in a pool of hard core rap, bright Euro techno, Koreanized hip hop, and disco-style electronic sounds. Subsequent idol acts like Shinhwa, TVXQ!, SHINee, and Big Bang also based their music in hip hop but mixed it with other musical styles. The girl groups that are popular now have their base in American hip hop and European techno. They have created "mutant

(Left) Rainbow / Source: DSP Media
(Right) Big Bang / Source: YG Entertainment

music," Lee said, by mixing up various musical sources and forms. "While Japanese pop differentiates itself from other styles with its use of funky Japanese rhythms and rock samplings," Lee elaborated, "the pop music of Korean idol groups uses strong dance beats, powerful rap flows, and sometimes complicated electronic factors—making it more dynamic than Japanese idol pop." Lee also said, "In terms of musical style, K-Pop has more global sounds and transnational images than J-Pop."

In December 2010, an NHK news program analyzed the reasons behind the popularity of Korean girl groups in Japan, saying that the catchy choruses and easy-to-copy group dances of the Korean girl groups were the most attractive aspects.

One of the most common features of K-Pop in the late 2000s is the repetitive, addictive chorus that "hooks" people into listening to the song again and again. "Tell Me" and "Nobody" by the Wonder Girls, "Lie" by Big Bang, "Sorry Sorry" by Super Junior, "Ring Ding Dong" by SHINee, and "Gee" and "Run Devil Run" by Girls' Generation all have brief but ear-catching hooks. The idol groups' synchronized dance steps are also a

KARA / Source: DSP Media

selling point, leading overseas K-Pop fans to copy them and upload videos of the resulting "cover dances" on YouTube.

In addition to music and dancing, fashion also plays a crucial role. Recently, there has been a fad among Japanese women to precisely copy the fashion of KARA and Girls' Generation, part of a phenomenon referred to as "costume play," or "cosplay." The media takes obvious advantage of this, offering information about the cosmetics and fashion used by Korean girl groups. The two aforementioned groups have successfully captured what young Japanese women want to emulate, creating a strong desire among Japanese fans to become just like the members of Korean girl groups.

The Versatility of Korean Stars

In an article on June 18, 2011, the English-language K-Pop information site Soompi.com said that 2NE1 "is by far one of the most versatile and talented groups in today's K-Pop." The four-member girl group is capable of working in a wide array of musical genres ranging from rap and hip hop to slow R&B. "Even with less TV promotions, compared to other mainstream artists, 2NE1 has been able to sustain popularity in Korea and beyond," the site noted, adding that "2NE1's versatility and top-notch talent, plus their colorful fashion, make them a top candidate to make strides in Europe."

Versatility among K-Pop artists has much to do with mixing global pop trends that are not particularly confined to any region or country. K-Pop music is created by leading producers and composers at major entertainment agencies, who are often armed with American and European pop-based techniques and mixing skills.

With K-Pop going more international, agencies have been working directly with world-renowned producers. A case in point is 2NE1's collaboration with Black Eyed Peas leader and producer will.i.am on the group's album. YG Entertainment head Yang Hyun-suk had a chance to introduce 2NE1's music video to the producer, who immediately accepted Yang's offer to work with the group.

will.i.am recently visited Korea to plan for future collaborations with YG Entertainment. He expressed his fascination with 2NE1 in various interviews and Tweets, describing them as "special" and a potential "super star across many countries."

"Hoot," "Genie," and "Run Devil Run" by Girls' Generation, "Nu Abo" by f(x), and "Replay" by SHINee were all created by composers from various

(Top) Yoo Young-jin has composed and written songs for various SM Entertainment artists, including H.O.T., BoA, TVXQ!, Super Junior, Girls' Generation, SHINee, and f(x).
Source: SM Entertainment
(Bottom) Teddy Park is a producer for YG Entertainment. He has worked on the albums of Big Bang and 2NE1.
Source: YG Entertainment

countries overseas. "Run Devil Run" was written by US-based Busbee, UK-based Alex James, and Sweden-based Kalle Engston. SM Entertainment officials said they have been searching for good music from around the world since the late 1990s. The agency has already built a global network of composers and publishing companies. It is known to examine thousands of overseas and domestic pop songs when making an idol group album.

Such collaborations illustrate that K-Pop has advanced to the point where it is digesting global trends of pop music and upgrading them to another level. NHK entertainment program producer Ishihara Shin said Korean pop music is based on American pop's powerful bass rhythms. The global impact of K-Pop has been further enhanced with diverse rhythms, vocals, and choreography.

Western Musicians Pay Attention to K-Pop

On an April 2011 visit to the country, veteran musician and producer Quincy Jones called Korean pop musicians "the best artists" in Asia. "I met with Tiger JK, BoA, and some other artists from YG Entertainment, and I thought they were amazing. I've been to China and Japan a lot of times before, but I think I can safely say that Korean artists are the best," Jones said during his short visit to Korea. Asked if Korean artists could succeed in the US pop market, he said he had no concerns about the Korean artists that he met. "From their choreography to their body language, all artists had an intrinsic nature for music, regardless of genre," he said. "I really met some of the best artists out there, and I want to say that their chances of succeeding are very high."

Quincy Jones

Teddy Riley, famous for writing Michael Jackson's super hit "Dangerous" and producing for Lady Gaga, said he was also stunned by the power of K-Pop music and the talent of Korean singers during his visit to Seoul in April 2011. Visiting

Teddy Riley

Korea to support his own girl group Rania, Riley dropped by the SBS music show *Inkigayo* where many other K-Pop stars were on stage. After seeing K-Pop artists such as TVXQ! and Big Bang perform, Riley said that he could understand why K-Pop music was so powerful. He noted that he had only ever heard about it from others, and that it made a profound impression on him when he saw it in person. Calling K-pop performances some of the best in the world, Riley expressed confidence in its ability to reach audiences in North and South America, Europe, and the rest of the world.

Globalized Star-Making System

In the past, pop and dance groups in Korea had a certain reputation. If the members were handsome or pretty, it was said, their singing or dancing skills would not match their looks. Even in groups, one member would have the main role of vocalist, while another member served as a figurehead.

This "formula" has been broken in recent years with the rise of groups such as TVXQ!, Girls' Generation, and Big Bang. In these groups, each individual member possesses his or own appeal and is capable of singing and dancing well.

Their unbeatable singing and dancing skills stem from the unique star-making systems created by the local entertainment industry, especially since the early 2000s. Major agencies in Korea like SM Entertainment, YG Entertainment, and JYP Entertainment have set up the so-called "total management strategy" to integrate all areas of discovering, nurturing, and promoting stars. Music marketing and promotion, compositions, arrangements, choreography, and fashion coordination are all planned and managed under an integrated management system.

The Korean Entertainment Agency's Star Development Process

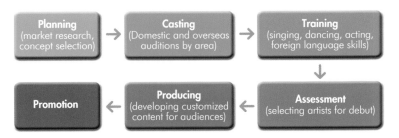

Aspiring teenaged singers practice their singing and dancing.

In particular, these agencies are famous for using exclusive, all-in-one training programs for aspiring idols. They select trainees through regular or sporadic auditions or team up with television shows for public auditions. Sun of the Wonder Girls and three members of 2PM were selected as trainees by JYP Entertainment through an audition collaboration with SBS.

After winning a fierce competition against numerous other aspiring stars at an audition, Korean idols generally go through years of training in singing, dancing, foreign language skills, and fitness. Even if one gets to join an entertainment agency as a trainee, there is no guarantee that he or she will survive the competition against other trainees and sign a contract with the company. It took an average of more than five years for the nine members of Girls' Generation to get where they are now.

Sandy Monteiro, Southeast Asia president of Universal Music Group International, which claims to be the largest distributor of K-Pop, said he was surprised when he visited a Korean entertainment agency and saw that several aspiring pop stars danced for six hours non-stop every day. "That doesn't happen anywhere else in the world," Monteiro said in an interview. "When I first met BEAST, they were just a bunch of boys, but I could see them change from boys to stars in front of my eyes."

Three Major Figures Behind
K-Pop's Global Power

Lee Soo-man, Chairman of
SM Entertainment

Lee Soo-man

Lee Soo-man is founder and producer for SM Entertainment, home to such globally recognized star acts as Kangta, BoA, TVXQ!, Super Junior, Girls' Generation, SHINee, and f(x). Lee masterminded the current management system of Korea's entertainment industry, contributing significantly to the expansion of K-Pop and the Korean Wave for the past 15 years. SM Entertainment works to produce high-quality global content with a training and production system that encompasses all areas of the act's music and style. SM Entertainment has also established overseas branches in China and Japan, searching for Asian talents with great potential to develop into world stars. The major characteristics of SM Entertainment artists like TVXQ!, Super Junior, Girls' Generation, and SHINee are their professionalism and charisma. As a result, they command a broad global fan base.

(Left) Girls' Generation
(Right) Super Junior
Source: SM Entertainment

Park Jin-young, CEO of JYP Entertainment

Park Jin-young

Park Jin-young began as a singer in 1994, having spent his childhood in New York. With the ability to write lyrics and melodies and dance in an unusual wardrobe, Park enjoyed success as a singer throughout the 1990s. He went on to begin another chapter in his career as a successful record producer, nurturing g.o.d., 2PM, and the Wonder Girls into top acts. Park has since expanded JYP Entertainment with the opening of a US office in New York in 2007 and a Chinese office in Beijing in 2008. The music of JYP Entertainment artists is known for its strong popular appeal, with songs targeting not only the teen audience but people in their twenties and thirties. The hit songs are notable for their distinctive concepts.

Yang Hyun-suk

As the 2000s began, producers started playing a bigger role in making pop stars. Yang Hyun-suk was a pioneer in this regard. As a member of Seo Taeji & Boys in the 1990s, his role was to give the group's music a hip-hop touch with rapping and choreography. After the group disbanded, Yang began his career as a producer for Keep Six and Young Turks Club. In the late 1990s, Yang set his musical focus on hip hop, producing the acts 1TYM and Jinusean. The "YG family" includes Seven, Big Bang, Gummy, and 2NE1. Most songs by YG artists are composed by Teddy, who does an effective job of matching hard-core "black music" based on hip hop and R&B with melodies and beats that have mass appeal. The music tends to be sophisticated, fun, and free-spirited.

Yang Hyun-suk, CEO of YG Entertainment

(Left) Big Bang
(Right) 2NE1 / Source: YG Entertainment

(Left) Wonder Girls
(Right) 2PM
Source: JYP Entertainment

Social Media Enables Rapid Spread

The rapid growth of social media has allowed a wide range of music to be shared around the globe through individuals and their friends. This stands in contrast with the traditional media approach, with its focus on the one-way introduction of mainstream music. Through the more than 600 million users of Facebook, songs can travel anywhere with a click of the "like" button among friends, and the increased distribution can lead naturally to consumption of this music. This has enabled Korean music to reach all markets of the world.

Although Korean pop music and singers started to enjoy meaningful international attention in the late 1990s, the K-Pop boom was limited somewhat to East and Southeast Asia. But as social networking services (SNS) hit the mainstream and enabled people to share music, photos, and videos globally, K-Pop began spreading rapidly among people seeking something new and different.

SM Entertainment executive director Jeong Chang-hwan said that while Asian pop music had previously faced excessive barriers to exposure in the Western world, it broke through in the wake of the social media boom. "SNS has enabled non-Western music to reach the world in a single click," he said. "Asian music has seized that chance."

When it comes to population size, no region can beat Asia, which allows for the largest of hit counts on Internet video clips. So far, Southeast Asia and China have yet to bring their pop music to a world audience, Jeong noted, adding that Japan focused only on its local market, the world's second largest market of pop music. In contrast, Korea has a very small local market, which had led Korean entertainers to look outside. "K-Pop used to be categorized as Asian music, but now it is a global genre," Jeong said.

A report by a private think tank also attributed the Neo-Korean Wave driven by K-Pop to the growth of SNS, including the video-sharing site YouTube. "Consumers can easily search and watch various videos and performances by artists on YouTube, including official music videos provided by entertainment agencies," the report noted. "With the introduction of the subtitle service in 2008 and audio transcription service in 2009, language barriers have been reduced as well." YouTube videos not only include stage performances by K-Pop stars but also footage of them dancing in their trainee days and speaking on TV shows, helping to prove that they have real talent.

Wonder Girls' "Nobody" Promoted by US Power Blogger

Perez Hilton, a powerful US blogger and television personality, is known for blog posts about entertainment industry gossip. His site, perezhilton.com, attracts an average of 1.5 million visitors each month and was ranked 34th by Billboard among methods for promoting music to the world. Hilton uploaded the Wonder Girls' music video "Nobody" on September 22, 2008, calling it "fab." The video clip was seen by America's largest entertainment agency, the Creative Artists Agency, and the girl group's contract with CAA led to inroads into the US pop market.

The Wonder Girls' "Nobody" video uploaded on perezhilton.com

The music video for "The Boys" by Girls' Generations was uploaded to SMTown's YouTube channel on October 2011. Within ten days, it had drawn more than 15 million hits and was ranked third in the "Most Watched" category for world music. Once uploaded to YouTube, K-Pop content is then shared through other SNS including Twitter, Facebook, blogs, and fan community sites, which has served to accelerate the K-Pop fever.

This phenomenon was noted by *Time Magazine* in an article on August 26, 2010. "Korean artists are bypassing traditional outlets like radio and television, aggressively steering their efforts to go international via the Internet," Bernie Cho, president of DFSB Kollective, was quoted by the article as saying. The company is a Seoul-based agency specializing in the international marketing of Korean pop acts.

YouTube's role in promoting K-Pop is not confined to promotion and the spreading of music. In an era when YouTube is a major source of music,

Official YouTube Channels of
YG Entertainment (Top) and
SM Entertainment (Bottom)

Young people from around the world show off their K-Pop cover dances.

musical content includes not only audio aspects but also visuals that flow and tell a story. Instead of depending solely on the lyrics, which present limitations owing to language differences, the K-Pop of today puts more weight on visual components like choreography and fashion. The so-called "MTV generation" of music has combined with YouTube to boost the spread at a much broader scale of audience around the world. People no longer simply watch music videos by pop stars; they copy them and make their own content to upload to the Internet. Easy to sing along with, K-Pop stands out among the other pop genres of the world in this dynamic. This is why there are so many K-Pop "cover dance" videos.

Chapter Three

HISTORY OF K-POP

This chapter offers a basic overview of the history of K-Pop, as well as an account of how its strengths, including transnationality and the versatility of its artists, were shaped by the history and culture of Korean pop music. Korean culture—not only in music but in all fields—was open and oriented toward the Western world through the 20th century. Today, the world has started paying attention to Korean contemporary culture. This chapter will look at how the interaction between Korean culture and Western influences led to K-Pop's current popularity.

Birth of Korean Pop Music (1885–1944)

In talking about the birth of K-Pop, it is necessary to examine the Korean historical and social context. In 1985, US missionary Henry Appenzeller started providing hymns and folk songs to Koreans at Pai Chai Academy. The songs, which evolved from hymns and foreign folk songs, were called "Changga" in Korean. Most Changga were adapted from the melodies of American or British folk songs.

"Shimcheongga," a representative example of the Changga, was adapted from the US folk ballad "My Darling Clementine" — using the same melody, but with Korean lyrics. The Northern Irish folk song "Londonderry Air" was also transformed into a Changga under the title of "Danny Boy." As most early Changga originated from Western melodies and forms, they tended to express views in favor of foreign powers and the enlightenment movement then under way in Korea. Over the same period, the country's Joseon Dynasty (1392–1910) was coming to an end under Japanese colonization (1910–1948).

(Top) Album issued by Columbia Records, one of the top record companies during the Japanese occupation
(Bottom) An LP by Lee Nan-young containing the hit song "Tears of Mokpo"

During the colonial period, the occupying Japanese forces confiscated private collections of Changga and published Changga textbooks to increase their influence over Korea. The Korean people's resistance to the occupation intensified and Korean pop started to burgeon in earnest over the course of the March 1 Independence Movement in 1919. "Huimangga (Song of Hope)" was one of the most popular songs sung among the Korean people in the hopes that the country's sovereignty would be restored. From this time on, the Changga would assume a major place in Korean popular music.

According to academic data, the first Korean pop album was *Yi Pungjin Sewol* (*This Tumultuous Time*), released in 1925 by Park Chae-seon and Lee Ryu-saek. This collection consisted of translated versions of Japanese pop songs. The first Korean-made pop song was "*Nakhwayusu* (*Fallen Blossoms on Running Water*)," recorded by Lee Jeong-suk in 1929. In the 1920s, most Korean popular music was going through a developmental stage as it went from translated versions of foreign songs to original compositions by Korean artists.

It was also during the period of Japanese colonization that another popular Korean genre, called "trot," took shape. Greatly influenced by Japan's enka songs, trot songs were a major trend in the early days of Korean pop history.

Korean War and US Influence (1945–1959)

Korean popular music went through a chaotic transitional period after the nation was finally freed after 36 years of Japanese occupation in 1945. Soon, the Korean Peninsula was divided in two—the anti-communist South and the communist North. This was followed by the Korean War, which started in 1950. Within just a few years of liberation, Koreans had to face the pains and sorrows of the war, which they sang about in many songs.

Although the Korean War caused astronomical damage to the nation, it also opened up a new chapter in Korean popular music history. New forms of music, mostly influenced by Western music, began mushrooming.

With a great number of US troops stationed in South Korea, new American pop music was introduced to Koreans as a matter of course. Performing groups from the United Service Organizations (USO) frequently visited

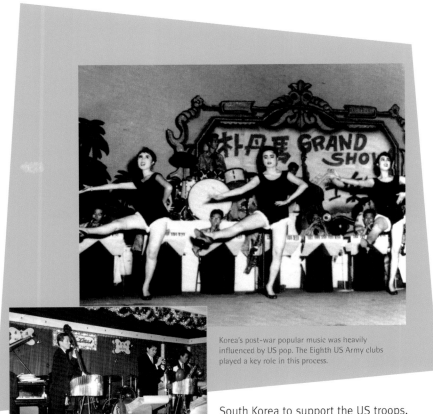

Korea's post-war popular music was heavily influenced by US pop. The Eighth US Army clubs played a key role in this process.

South Korea to support the US troops. Superstars like Nat King Cole, Marilyn Monroe, and Louis Armstrong held shows in South Korea, creating major buzz among the Korean people. In 1957, the US forces began their radio service, American Forces Korea Network (now AFN-Korea). This station would play a leading role in importing American pop culture.

During this period, the US influence on Korean pop took two forms— a major shift in musical style from the pentatonic scale to the Western heptachord, and the creation of Korean pop music modeled on Western pop. These trends are reflected in songs like "Shoe Shine Boy," a particularly

Americanized piece with its use of blues elements and swing rhythms.

It was at this time that the United States Information Service first began holding open auditions to recruit session musicians to perform at US army clubs. Since the local entertainment industry was a barren landscape at the time, skilled Korean singers looked to perform for the Eighth US Army. This was also a good means for Korean singers to earn money. The shows at the Eighth US Army became so popular that there were fully 264 clubs at one point. Earnings by Korean entertainers at shows for the US military reached as much as $1.2 million a year, which was almost equivalent to the total value of all South Korean exports at the time.

To pass the difficult auditions held by the US authorities, Korean singers put great efforts into mimicking the latest hit US songs. Shows at the Eighth US Army saw a diverse repertoire including country, rhythm and blues, and rock 'n' roll, based on jazz sessions. The US army clubs opened up a gateway for Korean artists to gain exposure to Western pop music and process it into the creation of Korean pop music.

The First Renaissance (1960–1969)

With the year 1960, Korean society met with rapid change. As the devastation and damage of the Korean War went through a process of healing in 1960s, economic growth and urbanization literally drove the nation's industrialization. On the pop culture scene, private broadcasters were launched and radio dramas enjoyed popularity. It was in the 1960s that the Korean film industry experienced its first heyday. Overall, the 1960s in Korea represented an era that shaped the fundamental pillars of culture and society.

With the US military still stationed in South Korea, Korean musicians who had previously performed for soldiers at the Eighth US Army clubs began heading out to floor the Korean public in the 1960s. These artists include instrumentalists like Lee Bong-jo, Kim Dae-hwan, Kim Hee-gap, Shin Joong-hyun, and Kim Hong-tak; composers like Han Myeong-suk and Choi Hee-joon; and singers like Hyun Mi, Patti Kim, Yoon Bok-hee, and the Pearl Sisters.

In the mid-1960s, the Western pop music industry was swept away by the legendary British group The Beatles. The group's massive success and

Korean Singers Go Abroad in Early Days

Kim Sisters' first album reissued in Korea in 1964

Although there were few Korean singers releasing albums overseas before the 1990s or 2000s, some were active overseas decades ago.

From the late 1950s, female acts like the Kim Sisters, Patti Kim, and Yoon Bok-hee went into the US market after holding shows for the Eighth US Army. In 1959, the Kim Sisters went to Las Vegas and became the first Korean act to release an album in the US pop market. Among their songs was a cover of "Charlie Brown," which reached No.6 on the Billboard Single Chart.

The Kim Sisters appeared on TV programs like the *Ed Sullivan Show* and radio programs and held a US tour, visiting New York City, Washington, DC, Chicago, and Dallas. They even toured Europe, traveling to Rome, Paris, Venice, Madrid, Munich, London, and Monte Carlo. An article on their activities was printed in *Life* magazine.

Female singer Yoon Bok-hee formed a band, the Korea Kittens, in 1963 and performed in Southeast Asia and the United Kingdom. Vocalist Patti Kim, with the help the mania of their fans quickly spread around the globe, also reaching South Korea. With the increasing popularity of rock bands, the Japanese music industry created a new term: "elecki group sounds," from "electric group sounds." As this term crossed the sea to South Korea, people started to call it "group sound."

The Beatles boom led to many variations on "group sound" in the Korean pop industry. Prominent examples of this were the Add4 and the KeyBoys. The Add4 was Korea's first rock group, formed by guitarist Shin Joong-hyun in 1962. After giving a brief showcase at the Eighth US Army club, the

of an AFKN executive, was invited by Japan's NET-TV in 1960 to do a national tour in Japan. She was the first Korean singer to be officially invited by Japan since the liberation of Korea in 1945.

Singer Han Myeong-suk became a star with the 1961 song "The Boy in the Yellow Shirt." The song presented an entirely new musical style that was noticeably different from previous Korean pop songs. With a typical American country and

Patti Kim

The 1960s hit "The Boy in the Yellow Shirt"

western style, it became a hit not only in Korea but in Japan and Southeast Asia as well. A movie of the same name was exported to Taiwan and Thailand, and Southeast Asian tourists began purchasing the album on their visits to Korea. When French singer Yvette Giraud visited Korea for a concert in 1965, she sang the song at Seoul Civic Hall and recorded a version for her album. In 1972, Japanese singer Michiko Hamamura performed a remake of the song; her album sold 300,000 copies that year.

The first original rock album by the Add4, a group formed by "godfather of Korean rock" Shin Joong-hyun, was released in 1964.

group disbanded. But after a reunion in 1964, it released its debut album, which included Korea's first rock song, "Bitsogui Yeoin (The Woman in the Rain)." At Seoul Civic Hall in the Gwanghwamun neighborhood (the current location of the Sejong Center for the Performing Arts), "group sound competitions" were staged beginning in 1968. All kinds of professional and amateur bands took part, with the Add4 emerging victorious three times in the late 1960s and the KeyBoys once in 1971.

Thus the 1960s was a period of development and coexistence for various genres, with the emergence of standard pop singers among the Eighth US Army performers, the "trot" of Lee Mi-ja, and the country's first rock bands.

Folk Music Represents Youth Culture (1970–1979)

It was in the 1970s that the younger and older generation began clashing head-on in Korean pop culture, as the post-war generation born after the 1950s had a very different way of thinking from the older generation. The younger generation had grown up under US influence and preferred the US lifestyle, while the older generation had lived consistently under

The film *Gogo 70* focused on the "group sound" of the 1970s.

the pressures of Japanese rule and compulsory education. The term "youth culture" entered use during this time; it referred to the phenomenon of Korean youths expressing themselves through long hair, jeans, acoustic guitars, and folk music.

In the late 1960s, the world was in turmoil with the US fighting a losing battle in the Vietnam War and the anti-war movement spreading rapidly throughout the world. "Hippies" advocating peace, love, and sexual liberation led a youth movement in the 1960s, and hippie-influenced culture, including music, was imported into Korea. Folk and rock songs expressing opposition to the Vietnam War, including the Kingston Trio's "Where Have All The Flowers Gone?" and Peter, Paul & Mary's "Gone The Rainbow," were banned by the Korean government because they ran counter to South Korea's participation in the Vietnam War.

A majority of the time's Korean folk music was initiated by elite university students or those who had graduated from prestigious schools. These included Kim Min-ki and Cho Young-nam from Seoul National University, Yoon Hyung-joo and Lee Jang-hee from Yonsei University, and Kim Se-hwan from Kyung Hee University. They were different in that they had started doing music as a kind of hobby or part-time job, while their predecessors had mostly used the theater or US military performances as

Leaders in the 1970s Korean folk music boom:
(from left) Kim Se-hwan, Song Chang-shik, and Yoon Hyung-joo

platforms for their musical debut.

"The fact that they represented the elite in Korean society enabled them to import American liberalism and the latest pop culture a few steps ahead of the general public," wrote Lee Yeong-mi in her book *History of Korean Pop Music*. "It was also university students who readily adopted Korean youth culture and folk songs, because they were the only group with the pocket money, the drinks and cigarettes, the relationships, the English ability, the long hair, the spare time, and the acceptance by society." Honesty and liberal values were significant characteristics of folk songs in the 1970s.

Established and hosted by the broadcaster MBC in 1977, the University Music Competition was an open door for Korean youths to seek diversity and quality in pop music. This competition resulted in the emergence of similar youth music competitions like the Gangbyeon Song Festival.

Launched in 1977, the University Music Competition became a springboard for many young musicians.

Hahn Dae-soo: The Korean John Lennon

Singer-songwriter Hahn Dae-soo initiated the Korean hippie culture and folk music movement in earnest starting in the late 1960s. After spending his teenage years in the US and being influenced by Bob Dylan, Leonard Cohen, and John Lennon, Hahn returned home to begin performing modern folk music.

His song "Mul Jom Juso (Give Me Some Water)" became a youth anthem, and his influence led Korean youngsters to pick up acoustic guitars. Hahn's unique performing style—mumbling words as though quietly rasping, screaming at times, improvising guitar licks and powerful lyrics—came as quite a shock to ordinary Koreans. Those who were not used to this style directed harsh criticism of his way; at one point, his music was banned by the military government. This forced him into exile in New York, where he continued performing.

Under the more liberal atmosphere of the 1990s, Hahn's musical value was rediscovered as his early recordings were reissued on CD. More than 30 years after his debut, Hahn held his second solo concert in Korea in 2001. In 2008, Korean artists of the indie music scene honored Hahn's contribution to Korean music history with a tribute album, which included different versions of "Give Me Some Water."

Hahn is still actively working with jazz, rock, and experimental music. He has released more than ten studio albums.

Western Pop Enriches Korean Pop

Starting in the 1960s, nearly every kind of American and European pop music has been introduced to Korean audiences. Consequently, Western pop songs translated into Korean gained huge popularity.

Especially in the mid- and late 1960s, music cafés and live music clubs sprang up all over the Jongno and Myeong-dong neighborhoods in central Seoul, serving as the main driving force for the birth of Western pop in translation. One music café in Myeong-dong, called C'est Si Bon, was home to folk music stars who sang American and British folk songs, French chansons, and Italian canzoni with acoustic guitars and lyrics translated into Korean.

Cho Young-nam's translated version of Tom Jones' "Delilah" (1968) and the folk duo Twin Folio's Korean cover of Nana Mouskouri's "Me T'aspro Mou Mantil" (1969) at C'est Si Bon helped them gain popularity, especially after their performances began being broadcasted on television.

The list of translated songs in the 1970s is more diverse. These included not only songs from the US and the UK but also New Zealand, Spain, and Russia. Among the songs enjoying great popularity were "One Summer Night" and "Graduation Tears" by Hong Kong singer Chelsia Chen, and even "Anak," originally sung in Tagalog by Freddie Aguila of the Philippines.

Greek singer Nana Mouskouri was popular in Korea during the 1960s.

Cliff Richard returned to Korea 34 years after his 1969 performance.

Western musicians visited Korea from time to time, with tickets almost always sold out. The best-known example of a Western pop star craze among female Korean fans came when British singer Cliff Richard held a concert in Korea in 1969.

American pop had a very powerful influence on Korea through the 1980s. In that decade, many songs adopted Western pop rhythms: the funky beat of Cho Yong-pil's "Motchatgetda Kkoekkori (I Can't Find It)," the slow go-go of Lee Yong's "Forgotten Season," and the rhythm of Sanulim's "Love Is Too Bitter for Me."

"The US military's AFKN radio plays American pop more than 20 hours a day. A record shop in central Seoul's Gwanghwamun neighborhood sells 200 new pop records a week and 1,000 records a month. Even among the songs broadcast on local TV channels, 80 percent is American pop."
Dong-A Ilbo on October 10, 1978

"With its interesting lyrics and bouncy rhythms, Western pop music is shaping the mainstream of Korean pop. This is because South Korea is deeply influenced by global trends in pop music."
Kyunghyang Shinmun on August 30, 1982

From The Beatles to heavy metal, many different genres of music from many different countries have influenced Korean pop music in the past, enriching the content of K-Pop in the 21st century.

The Beatles were a worldwide sensation, and Korea was no exception. Their influence would result in the emergence of Korea's first generation of rock bands, known as "group sound."

Superstar Cho Yong-pil and the Ballad Era (1980–1989)

Called the "King of Pop" to this day, Cho Yong-pil was a top singer of the 1980s.

Singer Cho Yong-pil released his debut song "Dorawayo Busanhange (Come Back to Busan Port)" in 1975. After being driven out of the entertainment industry due to his involvement in a marijuana incident in 1977, it was thought he would soon be gone from the pop music scene. But his first album, *Chang Bakkui Yeoja* (The Woman Outside the Window), achieved massive success in March 1980. In June of that year, he held a solo concert at Carnegie Hall in New York, the first Korean artist ever to do so. During the same year, he swept the best composer, best song, and best singer awards of the television networks KBS, MBC, and TBC. He was invited by Japan's NHK network to hold a concert in 1983, and he attended an international music festival in Hong Kong with actor and singer Leslie Cheung in 1985.

In 1988, Cho sang "Seoul, Seoul, Seoul" in three languages—Korean, English, and Japanese—to celebrate the 1988 Seoul Olympic Games. Cho's music encompassed almost every kind of genre. From rock ballads to rhythmic dance to trot and even folk, he was able to adapt his musical style and lyrics to the tastes and trends of the general public.

In the late 1980s, one of the dominant music genres in Korean pop music was the ballad. Originally, ballads were folk songs or lyrical music written by poets and composers. In the modern sense, however, the ballad is a slow form of popular love song. With the smash success of Lee Gwang-jo's "Gakkai Hagien Neomu Meon Dangsin (You're Too Far Away to Get Close to)" in 1985, ballads became a popular form. Lee sold more than 300,000 copies of his album.

Lee Moon-se's "Nan Ajik Moreujanayo (I Don't Know It Yet)" was another huge hit in 1986. It was followed by "Ibyeol Iyagi (A Story of Parting)" in 1987 and "Gwanghwamun Yeonga (Gwanghwamun Love Song)" in 1988. Most of Lee's songs were written by the late composer Lee Young-hoon, whose work was revisited in the 2011 musical *Gwanghwamun Yeonga*. Ballad singer Byun Jin-sub's 1988 hit "Hollo Doendaneun Geot (Being All By Myself)" contributed decisively to establishing the pop ballad as a mainstay of Korean pop music. Another song by Byun, "Sungnyeoege (To My Lady)," was also successful, and a string of popular ballads led to his earning the nickname of the "Prince of Ballads" in Korea.

Balladeer Lee Moon-se emerged in the late 1980s.

The ballad trend continued on into the 1990s with hits by Shin Seung-hun and Lee Seung-hwan.

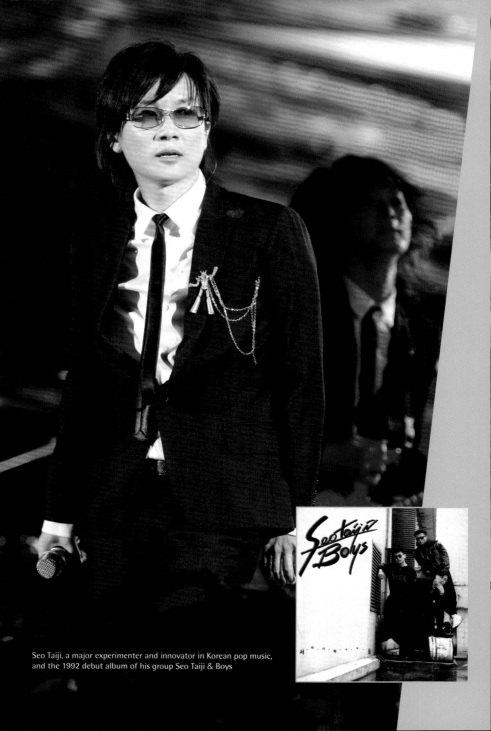

Seo Taiji, a major experimenter and innovator in Korean pop music, and the 1992 debut album of his group Seo Taiji & Boys

Seo Taiji & Boys Open New Chapter (1990–1999)

As the ballad boom was coming to an end in the early 1990s, a "new generation wave" started to hit Korea with the rise of the male trio Seo Taiji & Boys. Creative and new forms of pop music began flourishing, and dance music also enjoyed a great advancement in both quantity and quality. Together, this contributed to a golden age for the Korean music industry in the 1990s.

Seo Taiji & Boys debuted in 1992 on an MBC show featuring new artists performing in front of a panel of judges. The trio's song "Nan Arayo (I Know)" received the lowest score in the history of the program. Still, it did not take long for the band's unique and unprecedented musical style and fashion to dominate Korean pop music.

Formerly a bassist with the rock band Sinawe, Seo wrote "Nan Arayo" with a mixture of rap, plaintive lyrics, and heavy metal sounds. As this combined with the flamboyant choreography of the other two members, Yang Hyun-suk and Lee Juno, the band enjoyed a meteoric ascent to fame. Their fashion was another major focus of interest: teenagers copied the style with oversized jeans and T-shirts with the labels attached.

In 1993, Seo Taiji & Boys released a completely different style of music with their second album, *Hayeoga*. The title track featured a melody performed on the *taepyeongso*, Korea's traditional conical oboe, together with beatboxing.

As rap soared in popularity, other acts began adopting hip hop styles. The duo Deux debuted in 1993 and quickly became a pioneering force in Korean hip hop music. This was followed in the late 1990s by other hip hop acts like Jinusean, 1TYM, and Drunken Tiger.

Hip hop acts Jinusean (Left)
and 1TYM (Right)
Source: YG Entertainment

The huge popularity of Seo Taiji & Boys led the music industry to recognize teenagers as a new audience demographic. With the mass media enjoying the growing power of Korean teenagers, the music industry shifted its focus toward teen-centered pop music in the 1990s. From the middle part of the decade, this fundamental change served as a stepping stone for the birth of idol groups.

With the 1995 debut of the male idol quintet H.O.T., the K-Pop scene truly began to be dominated by teen-centered boy and girl groups. Formed by SM Entertainment, H.O.T. became a major influence on the future of boy bands. Entertainment agencies began developing their own "star-making systems," which would lead to the debuts of groups like Sechs Kies, S.E.S., Fin.K.L, NRG, Taesaja, Shinhwa, and g.o.d.

In the late 1990s, a downturn for the local market all but forced first-generation idol groups to look for opportunities in overseas markets. Just one year after the Korean economy was hit by the Asian financial crisis in 1997, H.O.T. had its first Chinese album. The boy band was able to

The first generation of Korean idol groups:
(clockwise from top left)
Shinhwa, Fin.K.L, S.E.S.

survive in a slumping Korean
music industry by digitizing its
music and courting the larger
Chinese audience.

While mainstream pop music was undergoing qualitative and quantitative change and development, indie music was also beginning to blossom in Korea, starting in the neighborhood around Seoul's Hongik University (popularly known as "Hongdae"). The Hongdae rock club Drug (now DGBD) played a crucial role in promoting indie music: indie bands like Crying Nut and Yellow Kitchen performed there starting in the mid-1990s. As Drug gained popularity, the neighborhood as a whole saw an increasing number of live clubs with a diverse range of bands playing punk, hard rock, heavy metal, blues, alternative rock, and techno.

Punk acts like Pipi Band and Crying Nut caught the attention of the public. With the 1995 song "Annyeonghaseyo (Hello)" from its debut album *Cultural Revolution* and the 1997 song "Ttalgi (Strawberry)" from

Punk bands Crying Nut (Left) and Pipi Band (Right)

Evolution, Pipi Band showed off vocalist Lee Yun-jeong's rebellious singing style and the band's cynical stance on mainstream pop music to strong effect. Crying Nut's "Mal Dallija (Let's Ride a Horse)" enjoyed such great popularity in 1996 that the song became a karaoke staple.

K-Pop Goes Global (2000–2010)

Many of the first-generation idol groups popular in the mid-1990s either disbanded in a few years or stopped performing together. Sechs Kies officially disbanded in 2000, H.O.T. in 2001, S.E.S. in 2002. The sextets Shinhwa and g.o.d. have not announced their disbanding, but also haven't performed together for some time.

Aging was the biggest reason for their decision. Moreover, most did not have strategies for maintaining competitiveness in the pop music market. Because the idol groups formed in the mid-1990s were developed almost exclusively by entertainment agencies, they did not have much chance to develop their own style of music. Their musical skills and talents were not enough to keep them afloat.

Although groups like H.O.T. were successful in attracting Chinese fans, their popularity did not last into the long term due to factors such as rampant pirating of CDs and policies for cultural protection by the Chinese authorities.

For this reason, major entertainment agencies have begun setting long-term strategies for reaching overseas markets. This includes the establishment of overseas offices and localization efforts aimed at better tailoring Korean artists to the tastes of young people around the world.

While the popularity of idol groups faded somewhat in the early 2000s, the female singer BoA made her debut and became sensation in Japan.

(Top) Corner dedicated to BoA's 22nd single, "Sweet Impact," at the Shibuya branch of HMV, Japan's largest music retailer (Bottom) Rain is active on a global stage as a singer and actor.

In 2002, she topped Japan's Oricon single chart with the song "ID: Peace B," two years after her Korea debut in 2000. Although many Korean pop musicians had expanded their reach to the Japanese pop market, none had ever hit No. 1 on the Oricon chart. In this sense, BoA's success was seen as revolutionary.

Even before her debut, BoA was receiving customized training to target the Japanese pop market. No sooner had her agency scouted her than it was helping her to develop her Japanese language skills, and her contract with the major music label avex greatly contributed to promoting her version of K-Pop in the Japanese music industry. Her Japanese debut *Listen To My Heart* sold 1.3 million copies in 2002, while her follow-up album *Valenti* sold the same number in 2003, and the third album, *No. 1*, sold 1.4

Concert-goers at a performance by the Korean boy band Super Junior
Source: SM Entertainment

million copies in 2004. All of this success led to her being honored with Japan's prestigious Golden Disc Award.

Singer and actor Rain's influence on overseas fans was strong as well. He drew an audience of 40,000 to a November 2005 concert in Beijing and was selected as the most anticipated Hallyu star by CNN.

Since the mid-2000s, not only solo acts like BoA and Rain but also second-generation idol groups have been able to appeal strongly to Asian audiences thanks to better musical strategies, performances, and marketing. Following the emergence of TVXQ!, groups like Big Bang, Super Junior, SHINee, 2PM, and 2AM each made their debut in the period from 2005 to 2008. Girl groups like the Wonder Girls, Girls' Generation, KARA, 2NE1, and f(x) further spurred on the mania for Korean idol groups.

The biggest difference between current K-Pop idols and those of the mid-1990s and early 2000s lies in the individual capabilities of the groups' members. Following the strategic outlines of their entertainment agencies, the individual members have played up their unique personality traits.

In addition to adding more talented performers, another strategy for helping idol groups reach overseas audiences more effectively has been the inclusion of members from other countries. Nicole from KARA and Tiffany and Jessica from Girls' Generation are Korean-American. In the girl

Digitization Helps K-Pop Go Global

The increasingly wide use of the Internet by the general public starting around 2000 and the introduction of the MP3 player have led to a sea change in the production, distribution, and consumption of K-Pop.

More and more people have started to buy digitized pop music files rather than heading to an offline record store to pick up their favorite CDs. According to data from the South Korean Ministry of Culture, Sports and Tourism, the local digital music industry has grown exponentially since 2000, overtaking the offline sector in 2003. In 2010, the digital music market was about seven times larger than the offline market.

As consumption patterns shifted from the purchasing of entire CDs to the purchasing of individual songs online, K-Pop musicians also changed the way they produced music. K-Pop

The iTunes store is an online sales outlet with the world's largest distribution of music.

group f(x), Amber is Taiwanese-American, and Victoria is Chinese. Nichkhun from 2PM is Thai-American, and Chinese Jia and Fei of miss A represents their group's multicultural aspect. Agencies hold auditions all around the world, attracting a flood of non-Koreans hoping to become K-Pop stars.

K-Pop is now spreading throughout Europe and the US, with many fans showing up at K-Pop concerts, cheering at the airport when K-Pop stars arrive, and organizing flash mobs to request more K-Pop concerts in their cities.

---

artists—especially those who debuted after 2000—began debuting with singles or mini-albums rather than full studio albums.

With the shortening of their recording activities into just a few singles, K-Pop idol groups had to attract popularity in a shorter period of time. This is one of the reasons for the repetitive, addictive chorus designed to "hook" people.

Because the audience for K-Pop was especially young and global, it was natural that Korean singers would upload their digital singles through the official YouTube channels of their respective agencies. Soon, the explosive success of these video clips would demonstrate K-Pop's worldwide popularity.

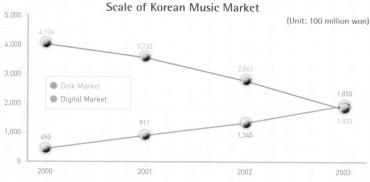

Scale of Korean Music Market

(Unit: 100 million won)

- Disk Market
- Digital Market

Year	Disk Market	Digital Market
2000	4,104	450
2001	3,733	911
2002	2,861	1,340
2003	1,850	1,833

(Data: South Korean Ministry of Culture, Sports and Tourism; Music Industry Association of Korea)

Chapter Four

THE MOST POPULAR
K-POP ARTISTS

This chapter introduces some of the most popular K-Pop acts. Although the K-Pop songs that are currently enjoying popularity overseas are mostly dance tracks by idol groups, pop music in Korea includes a far more diverse range of genres. Since emerging on the scene in the 1980s, the ballad has been beloved by audiences from all different age groups. R&B arrived with the trio Solid in the mid-1990s and went on to enjoy great popularity. In the 2000s, music by black artists developed into a mainstream style with adherents all over the world, and Korea was no exception. Since its beginnings in the 1990s with Hyun Jin-young and Deux, Korean hip hop has come to develop a more loyal fan base than any other genre. Korean rock went through something of a dry spell after its boom years in the 1960s and 1970s before gaining a new lease on life in the 1990s through the indie scene. The following is an introduction to some of the major acts currently working in the aforementioned genres.

Idol Pop

Girls' Generation (2007–)

• Members: Taeyeon, Jessica, Sunny, Tiffany, Hyoyeon, Yuri, Sooyoung, Yoona, and Seohyun

Source: SM Entertainment

The group has set a major record by topping local music charts with every song since its 2007 debut "Into the New World." Their EP *Gee* (2009) enjoyed such huge popularity that local news reports referred to it as "Gee mania." Adding to their success with "Tell Me Your Wish," Girls' Generation has become a major presence among Korean girl groups targeting the global pop audience. The group's latest song, "The Boys," has met with a strong response not only in Asia but in the US, Europe, and South America since its October 2011 worldwide release.

Super Junior (2005–)

• Members: Leeteuk, Heechul, Hangeng, Yesung, Kangin, Shindong, Sungmin, Eunhyuk, Donghae, Siwon, Ryeowook, Kibum, and Kyuhyun

Super Junior is a thirteen-member all-around entertainer group. The outfit has been active in film, TV shows, musicals, and radio programs. A subunit, K.R.Y., has performed on the soundtrack of many TV series. In addition, there is a trot subunit called Super Junior-T and a China-targeted unit called Super Junior-M. Major songs like "Sorry Sorry" (2009) and "Bonamana" (2010) spent a long time perched atop the music charts in Asian countries. This group enjoys widespread popularity in the US, Europe, South America, and Central Asia.

Wonder Girls
(2007–)

• Members: Sun, Yenny, Sohee, Yubin, and Lim

The Wonder Girls arrived on the scene with their first studio album *The Wonder Years*, and the leadoff single "Tell Me" quickly became the first famous "hook song" in K-Pop—pulling listeners in with its short and catchy chorus. The song enjoyed tremendous popularity, crowning the weekly online chart for eight consecutive weeks. Students, police officers, and even soldiers copied the accompanying dance. Follow-up songs like "So Hot" and "Nobody" were also successful. After their first concert in 2009, the act went to the US and was invited to play 49 shows on the Jonas Brothers' national tour.

TVXQ! (2003–)

• Members: U-Know, Max

This group's simultaneous debut in the Korean and Japanese pop markets was said to mark the starting point for the Neo-Korean Wave. Beginning on small stages, the boy band succeeded in reaching the pinnacle of the Japanese

pop market in the late 2000s. The members are famous not only for their handsome looks and charismatic dancing but also for their great singing talent. TVXQ! has enjoyed continued worldwide popularity over the years, with its 2011 album *Keep Your Head Down* topping the charts in Korea, Japan, Taiwan, and Thailand.

KARA (2007-)

• Members: Gyu-ri, Seung-yeon, Hara, Nicole, and Jiyoung

The members of KARA present a "girl next door" image. Since topping the local TV music charts with "Honey" in 2009, the idol group has enjoyed continued popularity with such songs as "Mister" and "Lupin," the second of which in particular marked a departure from the typical "good girl" image with its provocative lyrics and powerful sound. In a unique feat, KARA was already topping Thailand's Asian pop charts in its early days despite not promoting themselves overseas. In Japan, its debut single reached the Top 10 on the Oricon weekly single chart.

Big Bang (2006–)

• Members: G-Dragon, Taeyang, T.O.P, Daesung, and Seungri

Big Bang is arguably one of the most distinctive idol groups that has appeared since 2000. The five members possess outstanding musical skills, writing music and lyrics for their songs and producing them. In late 2010, G-Dragon and T.O.P formed a subunit, while Taeyang released five solo albums and Seungri put out the EP *V.V.I.P*. Even without official promotion in the US, Big Bang's mini album *Tonight* reached No.6 on the US iTunes chart, and the music video of its title track was watched one million times within two days of being released on YouTube.

2PM (2008–)

- Members: Junsu, Nichkhun, Taecyeon, Wooyoung, Junho, and Chansung

Targeting female music lovers with masculinity and powerful dance steps, 2PM got its name out through the cable channel Mnet's talent development

Source: JYP Entertainment

program *Yeolhyeol Nama* (*Hot Blooded Men*). The group made its debut with the song "10 Jeom Manjeome 10 Jeom (10 Points Out of 10)," which showcased the members' acrobatic dance styles. Their hit songs include "Again & Again" and "Heartbeat."

2NE1 (2009–)

- Members: Park Bom, Park Sandara, CL, and Kong Minji

This hip hop quartet is also known as the "female Big Bang." Prior to their debut, CL and Bom did background vocals for many singers, while Sandara was known from a KBS documentary series on her pursuit of a career in music. Minji was known as the granddaughter of Korean dancer Gong Ok-jin. Teaming up with Big Bang on the TV commercial background song "Lollipop," 2NE1 made a dazzling K-Pop debut in 2009. In contrast with other girl groups, whose members work hard to look pretty, the members of 2NE1 have successfully established their own unique qualities and personalities, with each pursuing a different fashion and offbeat style.

Source: YG Entertainment

SHINee (2008–)

• Members: Onew, Jonghyun, Key, Minho, and Taemin

SHINee is considered one of the youngest male idol groups. The group's soft, boyish image has stood in considerable contrast to the masculine and powerful image of 2PM. SHINee's hits include "Juliette" (2009), "Ring Ding

Source: SM Entertainment

Dong" (2009), and "Lucifer" (2010). In June 2011, more than 800 European fans gathered in front of Abbey Road Studios in London to catch a glimpse of SHINee. The group commemorated its Japanese debut with a performance at a closed reception where local media and European music industry professionals were invited to attend. It went on in November to become the first-ever Korean idol group to hold a solo concert in London.

f(x) (2009–)

• Members: Victoria, Amber, Luna, Sulli, and Krystal

This girl group has members from Korea, China, and the United States. Krystal is known as the younger sister of Jessica from Girls' Generation. Victoria, who comes from China, was featured in music videos by Super Junior and SHINee prior to her debut. Chinese-American Amber is known for her tomboyish style, while Sulli is currently involved in various activities, including MC duties for the SBS music show *Inkigayo*. Luna has been praised for her musical theater skills in performances of *Legally Blonde* and *Coyote Ugly*.

Source: SM Entertainment

BoA (2000–)

• Solo artist

BoA made her debut at the age of 13. Since then, she has had a successful musical career in both Korea and Japan. BoA is arguably the first Korean singer developed to target an overseas music market from the time of her debut. In Japan, she topped the Oricon weekly album chart with seven straight albums, including a greatest hits collection. Her ambitions have since turned to the US pop market: she released the digital single "Eat You Up" in 2008 and an English-language studio album, *BoA*, in 2009. She is set to make her Hollywood debut soon, casted in the leading role of the dance movie COBU 3D, which is scheduled to come out in 2012.

Source: SM Entertainment

Rain (2002–)

•Solo artist

Rain has many job titles. He is a pop and R&B singer, dancer, model, actor, businessman, and designer. Rain, whose real name is Jung Ji-hoon, made his debut with the album *Bad Guy*, with a title track that captured attention with his unusually masculine and smooth choreography, taking advantage of the artist's tall stature and muscles. His third album *It's Raining* sold over one million copies in Asia. Rain has now expanded the range of his activities to film, becoming the first Korean lead in a Hollywood movie with *Speed Racer* (2008) and the first Korean to win an MTV award for his role in the film *Ninja Assassin* (2009).

R&B and Ballads

Lena Park (1998–)

• Solo artist

Often referred as the "R&B Queen of Korea," LenaPark made her debut in 1998 in Korea with the album *Piece*, which sold more than 500,000 copies. Born and raised in the US, she did not grow up speaking Korean. But with the continued success of her second album *A Second Helping*, Park decided to pursue a musical career in Korea. In 2002, the song "Kkume (In a Dream)" from her fourth album *Op.4* became her biggest hit, and she appeared on the 2002 Korea/Japan World Cup album *Songs of Korea/Japan* with the Korean R&B duo Brown Eyes, the Japanese duo Chemistry, and the female Japanese singer Sowelu.

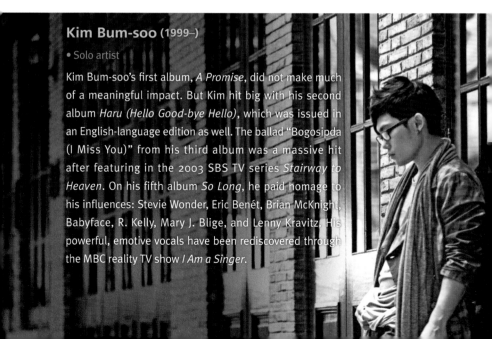

Kim Bum-soo (1999–)

• Solo artist

Kim Bum-soo's first album, *A Promise*, did not make much of a meaningful impact. But Kim hit big with his second album *Haru (Hello Good-bye Hello)*, which was issued in an English-language edition as well. The ballad "Bogosipda (I Miss You)" from his third album was a massive hit after featuring in the 2003 SBS TV series *Stairway to Heaven*. On his fifth album *So Long*, he paid homage to his influences: Stevie Wonder, Eric Benét, Brian McKnight, Babyface, R. Kelly, Mary J. Blige, and Lenny Kravitz. His powerful, emotive vocals have been rediscovered through the MBC reality TV show *I Am a Singer*.

Browneyed Soul (2003–)

- Members: Naul, Sung-hoon, Young-jun, and Jung-yup

Lead vocalist Naul formed the R&B quartet Browneyed Soul after the breakup of Brown Eyes, his R&B duo with Yoon Gun. Whereas that group had strong pop ballad leanings, Browneyed Soul features richer and deeper soul harmonies. The quartet made its debut with the album *Soul Free*, with the leadoff single "Did We Really Love Each Other" topping the local music charts that year. It took four years for the act's second album, *The Wind, The Sea, The Rain*, to emerge. When it did, it won them R&B honors at the Fifth Korean Music Awards in 2008.

SG Wannabe (2004–)

- Members: Kim Yong-jun, Lee Suk-hoon, and Kim Jin-ho

The members of SG Wannabe say they took their name because they wanted to be long remembered by the public like the US duo Simon & Garfunkel. With every album, they have enjoyed success, from their 2004 debut *SG Wanna Be+* to 2011's *SG Wannabe By SG Wannabe 7 Part 2*. In 2005 and 2007, they won top honors at the Korean Golden Disk Awards with "Crime and Punishment" and "Arirang," respectively, and "Partner for Life" won them the top award in the awards' digital category in 2006. Their third single collection *Precious* was also a hit in Japan, placing fifth on the Oricon daily chart upon its 2010 release.

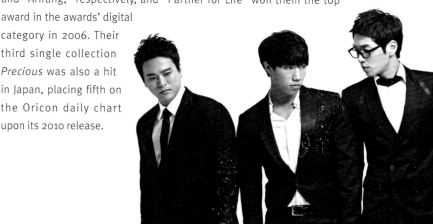

Hip Hop

Drunken Tiger (1999–)

• Solo artist/ensemble

A pioneer in the popularization of hip hop in Korea, Drunken Tiger was formed in the US by Tiger JK in the early 1990s, but made its official debut in 1999 with Tiger JK and DJ Shine. In 2005, DJ Shine left the group after participating on five albums. Today, Drunken Tiger refers not only to sole remaining member Tiger JK, who was active in the LA hip hop community during his high school days, but also to Tiger Clan, an assemblage of various cohorts from the hip hop world. Drunken Tiger's hip hop activities have expanded into the Movement Crew, the most widely known in Korea with acts like Epik High, Dynamic Duo, and LeeSsang.

Epik High (2003–)

• Members: Tablo, Mithra Jin, and DJ Tukutz

Describing their band and music in an interview, Epik High said they were "two MCs and one DJ. No genre, just music." Early on, the group did not earn much fame owing to hip hop's lack of popularity in Korea. The group started to gain

attention with its second album *High Society*. The leadoff track "Fly" helped the band sell 160,000 copies of its third album, 2005's *Swan Songs*. In 2009, the group held a world tour in Korea, Japan, and the United States. The group's basic orientation is hip hop and alternative hip hop. It is well known for its literate lyrics.

Dynamic Duo (2004–)

• Members: Choiza and Gaeko

Dynamic Duo formed in 2004 with the breakup of the hip hop group CB Mass, as members Gaeko and Choiza came together to create a new act. The pair's music is more audience-friendly compared to the rough, offbeat sounds of their previous group. Dynamic Duo released its debut album *Taxi Driver* in 2004. Its second album *Double Dynamite — Operating Manual* brought them Best Hip Hop Album honors at the Korean Popular Music Awards in 2005. In 2007, the members formed their own independent label, Amoeba Culture. After releasing the fourth album, *Last Days* (2008), they released a single collection that saw them working with other acts like the Wonder Girls and Supreme Team.

LeeSsang (2002–)

• Members: Gill and Garie

Gill and Gary, the pair that makes up LeeSsang, met as guest members of X-Teen. They performed with Honey Family before finally establishing the duo LeeSsang in 2002 and releasing an album. "*Rush*" from their first album *LeeSsang of Honey Family* showed a powerful pull with the public owing to its accessible melodies and the distinctive voice of featured female vocalist Jung In. The team's sixth album, 2009's *HEXAGONAL*, drew attention with a genre-blending array of featured performers including Lee Juck, Casker, and Chang Kiha and the Faces. Gill also works as a composer for other artists and served as general producer for Jung In's debut album.

Rock and Indie

YB (1997–)

• Members: Yoon Do-hyun, Heo Joon, Kim Jin-won, and Park Tae-hee

One of the most famous rock bands in Korea, YB was formed by vocalist Yoon Do-hyun, who started as a solo artist with his first album in 1995. The group made its debut with Yoon's second album in 1997. The first three albums received positive notice but didn't produce major hit songs. A big turning point for the band came during the Korea-Japan World Cup in 2002, when the band's powerful and rousing "Oh Pilseung Korea (Victorious Korea)" and "Arirang" became hugely popular. Musically, the band goes its own way rather than copying Western rock style.

Crying Nut (1995–)

• Members: Lee Sang-myun, Lee Sang-hyuk, Park Yoon-sik, Han Kyung-rok, and Kim In-soo

Crying Nut is Korea's first-generation punk band. After forming the group in 1993, the members won an audition at the leading Hondae club Drug in 1995. The group participated on the album *Our Nation Vol. 1*, the first indie music album released by Drug in 1996. Its debut album *Crying Nut* enjoyed a smash hit with the leadoff track "Let's Ride a Horse." In addition to its six studio albums, the group has been active in a range of other areas, featured in a movie and recording a song for the Korea Japan World Cup

Onnine Ibalgwan (1995–)

• Members: Lee Seok-won, Lee Neung-ryong, and Jeon Dae-jeong

The Korean modern rock pioneers in Onnine Ibalgwan were leading the indie boom. Lee Seok-won, who had led a modern rock club within Hitel's "Metal Community," appeared on a radio show introducing himself as the leader of a then-nonexistent band called "Onnine Ilbalgwan," or "Sister's Barbershop." The group formally took shape as interested people joined in. The act drew immediate media attention with its 1996 debut *Bidulgineun Haneurui Jwi (The Pigeon Is the Rat of the Skies)*, while their third collection, 2002's *Kkumui Papsong (Dream Pop Songs)*, became the first commercial hit in Korean indie music history.

Galaxy Express (2006–)

• Members: Park Jong-hyun, Lee Ju-hyun, and Kim Hee-gwon

Formed in 2006, the punk and garage rock band Galaxy Express is known for its work overseas: the group had a 2008 club tour in Tokyo and performed at the French music festival La Fête de la Musique, the 2009 Rock in Taichung Festival in Taiwan, and the 2010 Music Matters Festival in Hong Kong. As a member group in the Seoul Sonic Project, which aims to introduce Korean indie rock bands overseas through frequent concert performances, Galaxy Express toured Canada and the US in March 2011.

Korea's major **Music Festivals**

Incheon Pentaport Rock Festival

Launched in 2006, Pentaport can be called the event that truly opened up the popular music festival age in Korea. Its predecessor, 1999's Tripod Rock Festival, was suspended at its opening due to torrential rains, but it has brought a storm of attention from festival-hungry music fans with a lineup headed by star acts like Franz Ferdinand, The Black Eyed Peas, and Placebo. Taking part every summer in Incheon's Dream Park, Pentaport has become more than just a festival, establishing itself as a summer vacation spot for popular music fans.

Grand Mint Festival

The Grand Mint Festival, one of the country's rare indie music festivals, is known for its combination of nature and music, allowing visitors to enjoy a picnic while listening to performances at outdoor concert venues. Whereas previous festivals had mainly targeted male concert-goers, Grand Mint devised a lineup and venue to suit female fans, who are currently leading the way in the consumption of Korean popular music. The acts performing provide softer and more emotional music rather than powerful rock or heavy metal styles.

Jisan Valley Rock Festival

This festival was spun off from Pentaport in 2009 by Yellow9 Entertainment, which had previously been one of Pentaport's co-organizers. Like the early Pentaport events, it boasted a crowd-pleasing lineup of noted overseas musicians. It also formed a connection with Fuji Rock Festival, sharing participating acts. Thanks to these efforts, it rose in a very short time to sit alongside Pentaport as one of Korea's leading festivals.

Jarasum International Jazz Festival

Since first appearing in 2004, Jarasum International Jazz Festival has shattered the doubts of people who questioned whether Korea could hold a jazz festival, enjoying rapid growth with each passing year. Over 100,000 people visit every year, and 95 percent of the attendees are repeat visitors. This festival allows visitors to enjoy performances by gifted jazz musicians against the beautiful and comfortable natural backdrop of Jarasum, an island in Gapyeong County. This is considered one of the best festivals for couples and families to attend.

Where Is K-Pop Headed?

The question of whether overseas fans' consumption of Korean pop music and related Hallyu products will be sustainable has frequently surfaced since the early 2000s. The answer to that question can be found in the increasing coverage of K-Pop and Hallyu by foreign media.

On the Bloomberg TV program *Monocle*, MTV Asia vice president Ben Richardson said, "Korea as an entertainment exporter is, right now, very significant. Pretty much every market that MTV is in, I would say that Korean content is really driving ratings, program sales. It's really connecting to audiences." He went on to say, "Sometimes it's really hard to find one US hit that's going to work everywhere in multiple cultures. For a youth audience, it's really difficult. For us, Korean content is equal to anything that the US is producing right now."

Korea used to be associated with industrial brands such as Samsung and Hyundai. Now, it is being associated with K-Pop as a cultural brand. But, as noted before, this cultural brand was not built overnight. Even before becoming popular with the global audience under the "K-Pop" brand, Korean popular music was influenced greatly by the outside world, including Japan and the United States.

Accepting, copying, and reinterpreting various genres of Western and Eastern pop, Korean pop was able to build its own characteristics and qualities from the mid-1990s. Based on its competitive cultural content, Korea's pop music began traveling outward, as opposed to the inward flow of foreign pop music imports.

One thing that should be made clear here is that the globalization of K-Pop does not mean a one-way flow of musical exports. K-Pop is quite transnational in character, with songwriters, lyricists, choreographers, performers, and fans all coming from different countries and regions.

Songs by Girls' Generation and SHINee are written by US or European composers; the dances of Big Bang are designed by international choreographers; Central Asians and Latin Americans are crazy about Korean performers' singing and dancing; 2PM, which includes a Thai-American member in its lineup, and missA, which includes Chinese members, have drawn popularity in targeted Asian markets; and Korean entertainment agencies like SM Entertainment and JYP Entertainment have offices in China and the US to discover internationally talented musicians.

In addition to all this, developments in global communications tools have allowed K-Pop to be shared with the world at a much faster rate. The music

industry's growth engine has moved away from brick-and-mortar media like the CD and toward digital music sources and real-time streaming. Pop music listeners search for and recommend their favorite music on online sharing communities like Facebook and YouTube, which generates a viral effect. The advent of smartphones has changed not only the way people listen to music but the way they communicate with others through music. As a result, music and the public sphere of musical communication are not confined within the borders of Korea.

The popularity of K-Pop does not simply describe the phenomenon of a certain cultural product being consumed at a global scale. What should be noted is the way K-Pop has accepted the world's other forms of pop music to create a new, distinctive style, and the way it has led in turn to other imitations and transformations as it is enjoyed by audiences around the planet. This is a trend of cultural creation and appreciation that is taking place all over the world today, not only in Korea. And as long as that trend continues, K-Pop will be created and distributed through the various interactions and communications of the international community—a cultural phenomenon for the 21st century.

Further Reading

Books on Korean Pop Music

Berry, C., Mackintosh, J. D., Liscutin. N. (Eds) (2009) *Cultural Studies and Cultural Industries in Northeast Asia: What a Difference a Region Makes.* Hong Kong University Press

Craig, T.J., King, R. (Eds) (2002) *Global Goes Local: Popular Culture in Asia.* Vancouver: University of British Columbia Press.

Howard, K. (Ed) (2006) *Korean Pop Music: Riding the Wave.* BRILL/Global Oriental

Leto, J. (2011) *A Look at K-pop Boy Bands, Girl Groups and the Big Three Entertainment Labels.* Webster's Digital Services

Russell, M. J. (2008) *Pop Goes Korea: Behind the Revolution in Movies, Music, and Internet Culture.* Berkley: Stone Bridge Press

Websites on K-Pop

www.allkpop.com
www.soompi.com
www.kokokoreano.com
global.mnet.com
www.dkpopnews.net
www.enewsworld.net

www.gokpop.com
www.sarangkpop.com
www.seoulbeats.com
www.k-popped.com
www.popseoul.com
www.kpopmusic.com

Korean Music Festivals

Pentaport Rock Festival   www.pentaportrock.com
Jisan Valley Rock Festival   valleyrockfestival.mnet.com
Jarasum International Jazz Festival   www.jarasumjazz.com
Grand Mint Festival   www.grandmintfestival.com
Global Gathering   www.globalgatheringkorea.co.kr

Organizations

Korean Association of Phonogram Producers   www.kapp.or.kr
Korean Music Copyright Association   www.komca.or.kr

Agencies

SM Town   www.smtown.com
JYP Entertainment   www.jype.com
YG Entertainment   www.ygfamily.com
DFSB Kollective   www.dfsb.kr

CREDITS

Planner   Wi Tack-Whan
Writer   Kim Yoon-mi
Copyeditor Colin Mouat

Edited & Designed by   Seoul Selection

Photographs

Yonhap Photo 4, 6, 8, 16, 17, 18, 24, 25, 35, 37, 39, 40, 41, 45, 46, 55, 56, 57, 58, 59, 60, 61, 62, 67, 79, 82, 83, 86, 87, 88, 90, 91

University of Seoul Museum 48 (Top)

Mokpo Natural History Museum 48 (Bottom)